ARCADE

A R C A D E

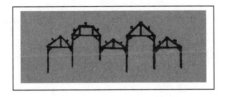

M A R C   W O O D W O R T H

Grove Press
New York

Published simultaneously in Canada
Printed in the United States of America

FIRST EDITION

Library of Congress Cataloging-in-Publication Data
Woodworth, Marc.
    Arcade / Marc Woodworth.
        p. cm.
    ISBN 0-8021-3877-2
        I. Title.
    PS3623.069 A89 2002
    811'.54—dc21

                                    2001040548

Design by Laura Hammond Hough

Grove Press
841 Broadway
New York, NY 10003

02 03 04 05   10 9 8 7 6 5 4 3 2 1

For Emma and Kodah

CONTENTS

ACKNOWLEDGMENTS

Berkshire Review: "Jerome's Dream"

The Paris Review: "Adrian Leverkühn's Song for the Clearwings," "Children and Cigarette," "The City from a Field," "The City from the Center," "Lovis Corinth at Walchensee"

Salmagundi: "Arcade," "Frieze," "Letter from Paris," "Ockham," "Sophia Tolstoy at Yasnaya Polyana"

Western Humanities Review: "An Uncut Scene from Herr Soma's Last Film," "A Letter from Ryder," "The Return" (as "Adam's Return")

Yankee: "The Heron"

The City for Paul Hockenos
"A Letter from Ryder" for Martin Pops
"Learning Las Vegas" for Rick Litvin
"Ockham" for William Brynteson
"For a Street Singer" for Mary Lou Lord
"Thaw" first read at Knockinaam Lodge, 22 December 1997

Much love and thanks to Bruce Woodworth; Jenny, Steve, Lori, and Josey Kirkland; Peter Hanson; and to my *Salmagundi* family: Robert and Peggy Boyers and Tom Lewis.

My gratitude to Richard Howard whose extraordinary attention and long-standing support are essential to my work as a writer.

I've been very fortunate to study with three poets who are gifted and giving teachers: Barry Goldensohn, Paul Nelson, and Frank Bidart.

Thanks to Jim Longenbach for his willingness to read this book in an earlier form and for his acute responses and suggestions.

I'm deeply grateful to Joan Bingham for her interest in this book and to Hillery Stone whose intelligence and generosity have made the process of publishing it such a pleasure. Thanks also to Zelimir Galjanic, Charles Rue Woods, and Michael Hornburg at Grove Press.

I'm grateful for the support and friendship of colleagues at Skidmore College and The New York State Summer Writers Institute.

Thanks to: Lucy Kaplansky and Rick Litvin for music, movies, talk, and travel; Samantha Dunn and Georgia English, writers whose friendship makes work and life possible; Nancy Peterson for being an ideal and enthusiastic reader; Michael Moore for being a supportive, steadfast friend; Joshi Radin, for calm and IZC and loving the creatures; Tara Jepson for goodness and so much help.

This book is for Emma who makes it all work, with help from K, N, B, B, S, M-M & B. I'm still thanking them . . .

FOREWORD:
A Note on Marc Woodworth's *Arcade*

The *site* of poetry has changed a number of times in our societies, as has the site of philosophy: when Aristotle gave lectures to the rows of listeners in the Stoa, that was a different settlement of the act of intelligence from those occasions when Socrates walked down to the Piraeus surrounded by his troop of eager young men; subsequently, it was sufficient for Sade to call his treatise *Philosophy in the Boudoir* for yet another dispensation to be evident.

The site of poetry has been even more volatile than that of philosophy: where poetry is made and where read (the study, the stage, the armchair, the garish beach by day and the gaslit park bench by night) has sustained a great many variations, a great many generic identifications too. Of course poetry *outdoors* has always been with us, but not comfortably so in modern times, when classroom strictures have prevailed. Besides our Ammons, the last really splendid open air poet I can think of was Émile Verhaeren, run over by a train in 1916; *hallucinated fields, tumultuous powers, tentacular towns*—those are merely the titles of his most famous books. And an analogous exteriority, call it the sweeping view, is what immediately strikes one about Marc Woodworth's *Arcade:* a gallery of fierce vocatives, a bird, a weed—whose woods these are I haven't a clue, these fields being anything but pastoral—then a sinister reservoir, and darkening them all that grand urban sequence "The City from a Field," "The Estranged City," "The City from the Center," "The City from the Air," "The Sorrowful City," "The Consoling City," so many more. This new poet—iconically, he calls the poem from which I most want to quote "The Poet in the Street"—is bound and determined to describe his fellow human beings *from without* as creatures living together, whether in groups or frayed from them:

. . . the world without a screen,
the men and buildings no longer defeated
by distance or the false physics
of some alien light, the world

where the deutsche mark drops,
a comet traces an arc of pale rose
over the city's alabaster center,
and the motiveless smokestacks

shadow the steeples from their stations
in outlying quarters, hung by day
with diesel smoke, lit all night
by a yolk-yellow incandescence.

Yes, Verhaeren is the readiest analogy (not influence) to come to mind as a precursor of this intensely public, densely *general* poetry. Not of course that Woodworth cannot muster or master the note of intimacy, the joys and sorrows of private life (just look at the poems for—"by"—Lovis Corinth, Albert Pinkham Ryder, Sophia Tolstoy). But Woodworth's spectacular note is struck *from without, from above, from afar.* This passionate voice is always one of address; if we wish to encounter the poet himself we can (readily) locate him in his apostrophe to others. I don't think the first person *singular* is ever used by Marc Woodworth to indicate the poet speaking in his own behalf, and if that is a kind of modesty it is also a version of pride, the vocative principle which readily confides itself to identity revealed otherwise than by a private *I.*

The burden, then, of this poet's responsibility rests (quite confidently, as I suggest) on his eloquence, his way of making us *see.* For him, as Conrad observes somewhere, the significance of an event or a place is not to be found within it, as within a nutshell, but *without,* enveloping the language that has generated it as a light generates a vapor. When Woodworth's old Adam returns to a "fallen" paradise, he moves easily where the trees "put off" and the landscape is reduced to essence, "shapes of clay and umber made plain"; in what are now seasons, he can see

> *. . . past the apple tree's trunk*
> *to a brook moaning only its original chord, unnamed, unnamable.*

The new poet must begin "the work of naming" all over again.

Richard Howard

I

The City

—after Frans Masereel

THE POET IN HIS GARRET

He has the accoutrements of the Romantic—
garret, moon and stars—
locked in a parallel happiness,
blind to the city's fixed grids,

dreaming of a nowhere,
void, apart from logic
and the steel of sparked wheels,
the footsore, faceless walkers. . . .

What is it he misses, dreaming?
All the average suffering
(it is not a strange city for that,
its unexceptional quotient of grief):

the legless pensioner knuckling his way
along the Something-Strasse
above the shrieking vowels of his greaseless cart;
the rape by the canal, remote,

unseen behind the sleeping factories,
their sooty chimneys free
from ash tonight, the girl's thigh
a pearl in the black hand

of her mug-faced criminal;
the hanged man declining
elegantly from the bedroom chandelier,
his face neither surprised nor weary

in his chosen death,
as if the complex verb of his life
dropped to the simple past,
recoiling from the new monstrosity;

the flower woman, babushka,
all tatters and the grime of wandering,
a face of beaten tin,
outside the chic nightclub—

she sees inside, as he does not,
dreaming in his room,
the swollen chests of men
under their waistcoats

the paltry bundles those fine wives make
in their husbands' sweating fists
as they dance the parquet floor
beneath the hissing promise of the gaslights. . . .

O city, you are dead to the poet,
this garret dreamer sucked aloft
by the cheap crescent of the moon,
the five-pointed longing of the cartoon stars.

The streets are full of lovers—
one stumbles slowly home,
his lips still stuck to her alabaster cheek,
in bliss, a bliss about to pass;

the elegist of snow who wishes
on each small point of white
drifting to its silent termination
against the trolley's fogged glass.

We are singing in the squares,
kissing women in their long gloves
on the rooftops of Kreutzberg,
the streets beneath lit by fireworks,

red and amber, the city stalled
in revery, the city a jewel
set between an old year and a new—
we are waiting for nothing,

all worlds known to us here
on the fuming winter pavement
or the frost-heavy streets,
our eyes level with the eyes

of those around us, our noses
buried in the divine feathers
of the augur's dark pigeons,
those fingers we once called our digits

finding a small, surprising warmth
in the pockets of our black clothes,
the rigid clefs of our ears alive
to the revolutions of the clock towers,

and the sentinel's shrill whistle
rising from the wooden platform
where the trams arrive and depart
far beneath the poet in his garret, lost to us.

THE CITY FROM A FIELD

He is looking at the city from a field,
    the flowers at his back elaborate symbols
      of some spurned reality:
    pinwheel semaphores, all petal and pistil,
the ghosts of spiked streetlights now sealed

and invisible in the urban tantric
    and this misremembered daylight.
      Only from this vantage—
    call it *the past*—does the streets'
multiform argument yield its false logic,

can the dialogue of smokestack and steeple sound audibly.
    Do you hear the singing of the distant revenants,
      see their somnambulant circuits,
    their routes buried like the tunnels of ants?
Their only meted fate is irreallty.

As seen from here, the men of reason pass unseeing
    the men of spirit in the boulevards,
      a warmth moving through a coolness.
    Even in the bustling streets and railway yards
these walkers disappear in a spell of edges

and the rapt geometries of the perfect planes
    of sun-gilt facades, the unbroken phalanx
      of tall windows adamantine,
    beautiful as this field's thwarted blue phlox,
even the architecture's run of miles, wane

in the distance as perspective collapses
    on its way to the unalterable, unreachable apex,
      and the biggest building on the block
    turns vaporous, a proof against its marble fact:
at this remove, the city as it is and will remain disappears.

THE ESTRANGED CITY

The city estranged from its makers, dead
and living, whispers its threats as we walk

the hard streets in twilight's bare shadow.
We are distinct and indistinguishable as the burlesque girls,

as stock in shop windows that we eye
on the unfamiliar but fully lit boulevards,

all the erotics of commodity displayed for the masses
and the men of means—the half mannequins white

as an imaginary wedding, trunks and limbs,
the headless fantasies of the body, all over the city.

We slip into the chocolate shop's inebriating haze of sugars
where the confectioner pours sweet tar into a human mold.

We find the unmarked door to Paradise
where we take even our wives to see the blackface minstrel

lift the wigged beauty, her kick revealing
well-groomed pubes chaste as an unwritten draft.

We leave the mills after our shift to the smell
of someone else's supper cooking that is also our own supper
        cooking,

our single coarse cap pulled down over our single brow
against the agitating chill of the new night breeze.

As we walk farther from the shining turbines
and the stammering factory's galvanized floor

we become our indistinct and insoluble selves,
each of us arriving at a door that is ours alone.

We meet at the cinema, drawn to the the sign
of the knife and the girl, the bright marquee

awash in neon above the circling spotlight;
we visit the dying aunt with lost cousins who bear our name,

uneasy with her once fashionable art, that brocade
of forgetting, some hidden lineage in the death room;

we drag the canal for the body of a whore or schoolgirl,
which we will not find until the sun, soot and red,

climbs the rungs of morning windows to peer
into cavernous streets we have named for our heroes.

When did the city exceed the grasp of its makers?
When did the number of bricks and the weight of stone,

the piles that rise and fall during each season of renewal
or decline, become incomprehensible? The unmapped alley,

home to seven rats, the rib cage of a horse, at night,
a pair of boys for sale . . . as if with enough time before us

we might recover each beautiful and tawdry thing
with an adequate flourish of newly coined terms,

dream of completion by naming each angel
whose tears darken cobbles in the city's clean center,

each monster who's drawn through the plazas and alleys
by the smell of leather from the forgotten district.

We imagine only what has left our sight
to quell the prodigality of even an ordinary night like this,

to calm our fears that the muscles gone to detritus
erecting the monuments, the now-crumbling chimneys,

the church steeples with their thin veneers of gold,
have served to make a world that is not ours,

one grown mindless and insupportable
in the ungoverned spaces beyond what we imagined.

THE CITY FROM THE CENTER

The workers labor in the emptied lot.
    The sweat of aluminum noon
        tempers their glinting picks and shovels
    in the half-dug dirt of the new foundation,
the layers where the past slept in oil and slate.

They turn and work in the crucible of the city,
    straining their muscles to complete
        the unsolved equation of renewal and decline
    abandoned by the architect purged of shale and soot
at his clean table far from this brute activity.

No one looks up at the tall cranes of iron,
    the crucifix and curtains of the empty windows,
        unreal above the protest of the steel and stone,
    the city's fan of standing buildings slowed
and emptied by the hunger of this pit of generation

from which the new city rises and every made thing's context
    changes, new relations, unthought of, unseen
        by the faceless walkers behind the bulwarks,
    who pass incurious this world of levels and lumber, the clean
fill, the spun rays that turn beneath the mason's cart.

It is the dead who will inhabit the stories still unbuilt,
    their offices now on floors of air, their desks at rest
        in ether, porous drawers of ink filled with nothing.
    The workers never see their buildings finished
or walk the polished marble, thralls instead to the economies of silt.

They are stalled in the making of your city,
        shuttled to the next foundation with their shovels
            but unavailable as Romantic ciphers
        for your fantasy of a righted world or as devils
in the nightmares you claim have made your children dirty.

Try to see them more abstractly, not sweat in the cotton
        of their thin shirts and burnt whiskers of ash,
            but backs and arms that turn to wings,
        beating toward no promised end, annihilating a specific past
once dense with meaning, the invention of generations now forgotten.

THE SORROWFUL CITY

These are the night streets of the sorrowful city
where we wail on the boulevards, inconsolable,

our arms outstretched, our once mute agonies
sounding now above the city's warning bells,

our unseen scars lighting the intentional darkness
brought on by our desire for despair,

each of us a new martyr without a feast day.
The lamps on querulous poles above our heads

should comfort us but are too bright
to accord with our dark, shapeless sorrows,

so we ignore them and step around their cones of light.
There are none outside this grief to track us;

nothing's remembered here—all's static,
everything merely recorded: a hammer beating another groove

into the metal ledger open to the current page
as sparks drop indecipherable from dark's anvil

leaving no trace of our wanderings
on the one true calibrated map of despair.

Wretched and naked, we minions are tripping
through the slums of self-exposure, our hands

limp as the wings of dead birds and the one shape
of sorrow—O—rounding our parched lips,

making our unabashed way down the streets
in full view of the gates and bars, the monuments and tenements,

the sound of our sorrow brought back to us by concrete,
that hard sound echoing beyond our understanding.

THE CITY FROM THE AIR

The broadsides float above the old city,
    fresh propaganda, clean white sheets
        curled and drifting downward,
    their printed sides facing the streets,
distributed by the vague breeze unequally.

A free fall of the meaningful,
    a windfall meaningless as snow,
        beautiful and illegible
    from the plane. We begin our slow
descent back to the world, the message stalled

above the mirage of the streets, the squares'
    traffic, windows full of bitter glass,
        all so far below us
    that we forget for now the crass
and fervent purpose of our writing on the air.

Long after these white pages have been ground
    to dust beneath the heels of men,
        read or unread, ignored
    or acted on, we will retain
the memory of the paper gliding down,

shimmering in the sun's vertical light,
    a thousand bright sheets on the wind,
        evanescent as new dreams,
    against dark rooftops and the river's bend,
emptied of the certain words we wrote.

THE CONSOLING CITY

Almost dusk. The streetlamps pose
their muted questions to the lost light,

tongues of gas above the sidewalks.
Each unhurried walker hears this dialogue

of division—day from night, the crush
of bodies from the hour's absolute solitude,

two hearts beating in every chest,
one fleshy and inert with familiarity, the other

a shadow heart unmarred by grieving,
adrift and unhinged, aquiver for the glow

contained by each tall window. For this hour,
you learn to narrate the city's story, a compline,

secular and half heard, your speech the voice
of cinders under a trolley's wheel

as it moves over streets newly dressed
by a darkness settling the elements

in their true and final order, simple
and obdurate. Oh, for that grace

of chiaroscuro, the regnant invisibility
of the oncoming night, sweetness

from the white petals of a closing flower
on the new breeze waking in the lindens,

lifting off the river, free of bearing now that night has come,
each of us dreaming our way from the plaza's

gray pavements to the perfect door,
imagined, still distant, we have not yet reached.

THE POET IN THE STREET

The writing he abandons—white words
fallen from the sky, frostbit
characters that lose their limbs
before they reach ground—

he has forgotten willingly;
now the world is before his eyes:
not the cinema of windows through which
he watched the city like a victim

but the world without a screen,
the men and buildings no longer defeated
by distance or the false physics
of some alien light, the world

where the deutsche mark drops,
a comet traces an arc of pale rose
over the city's alabaster center,
and the motiveless smokestacks

shadow the steeples from their stations
in outlying quarters, hung by day
with diesel smoke, lit all night
by a yolk-yellow incandescence.

Nothing is emblematic here,
no dirge from meaning's widow
in the unmoving assembly line's
machinery. Instead, there are lovers

behind the factory, and death
inside the faction that carries
the black flag of no clear party
past the closed theater.

His pen is at rest and he is awake,
the symbols of his vanity,
garret, moon, and stars, fallen
from his threadbare sleeves,

from his living hand,
not the automatic digits
of the imagined worker
or the porcelain leg

of a farm girl from the border
he waits to meet in the alley,
her face, flushed, a vivid oval
between her black hat and a scarf

wrapped tight under her chin.
Her stride is a beautiful import
so different from the scissoring
of the chorus line, a movement

from which she regains her body.
Even the silence between them
is welcome when it arrives
from the empty freight yards

and the daily-dragged canals
where they walk until daylight,
while all over the city
the kiss and the rape,

carnival and funeral,
a shooting and a birth,
the speech and the scream,
the starving dog and the well-fed.

And he is on the street,
no world closed to him now,
each tenement and shop vivid
with the inimitable, no desire

for dread replication or the sighing
perspectives of his high room,
missing nothing and forgetting nothing,
grateful to be broken back to this.

LOVIS CORINTH AT WALCHENSEE

The bodies line this lake of suicides.
I visit the locked shed
where lovers carve their summer oaths. Inside
the corpses gather. Drunk or mad,

some found their depth in these black waters.
Others, more sane than I,
lost to sorrows another month would cure,
took Goethe's road from Munich, pining

like stock Werthers for some pretty thing.
The Poet stopped to sketch
the church, then traveled on. I stay and train
my eye to read the lake's essay on death.

This September's page is blurred by sweat—
it's mortal weather. All
smells heightened: lakeweed, fir, and shit.
My body longs for the chaste air of fall,

but Germany spawns only a rank wind—
trenches filled with boys
and old men dying as they hold their ground. . . .
Still a painter, I stare down this shore

for stasis' sake and find in it *landscape*,
that old trope for calm,
until I see my larch slashing the lake
with its stiff spine, irradiating harm,

inking the water with its brutal sap.
What leaks from its branches
negates the lake's achievement, collapses
the crosshatched surface—its fine meniscus

articulating the desire of the wind—
with charnel depths
where corpses whisper, *rescind, rescind,*
and the currentless calm means nothing.

ADRIAN LEVERKÜHN'S SONG
FOR THE CLEARWINGS

The empire's train rolls west from Pressburg's heights;
I fall from sleep to sleep, dreaming of clearwings,
thousands, flying over Father's meadows,

their movement legato—a shimmer over staffs
of sweet grass, sweeter than any music
I could make now, past what's pure, past all belief

in unadulterated signs of love,
those signs that Father found in everything
God made: a butterfly, the linden grove,

pollen dust, pearling on a mussel shell. . . .
He tried too hard to read the world;
as if the Esmeralda's wing spots could reveal

Nature's design. He had it wrong.
His brand of faith made him see no more
than beauty where all was deception.

I now know things to be more random and exact—
last night, my Esmeralda, spoilt hothouse whore,
made me sick with joy between her legs. The act

wasn't for pleasure, or not for pleasure
of the kind I imagine most men go to women for.
Her sickroom had the odor of stale fear.

The unchanged sheets burned from her heat,
a half-dead bunch of feverfew sullied
the water in a blown-glass vase, the street

below her window teemed with Slavs
in a brute darkness cast there by the razed castle
high above the Danube's scrawled bass clef.

The brush of her brown arm a year ago
sent me reeling from her madam's house.
Since then, I've craved that touch: a slow,

poisonous yearning for defilement.
She told me she was ill—a kind of camouflage
like insects use to put off prey. I spent

myself on her despite the warning—
and there was nothing there to call nature,
in her fever screams, those pitch-black songs

that haunt my dreams of the false order
where we still gather under the linden
singing in round, *Es tönen die Lieder,*

while clearwings, *Hetaera Esmeralda,*
weave pure notes above the chastened grasses
and I know already what I haven't words to say:

There's nothing to hold back the increments
of desire that turn the world to ash,
the world unmade by the one monstrous art,

the one true song I am meant to write
of the raw place where the spirit starves
and the train passes beyond any city's light.

SOPHIA TOLSTOY
AT YASNAYA POLYANA

*I sat on the grave for a long time, then wandered about conversing silently with my
dead Lyovochka.*

                                   —Sophia Tolstoy, diary entry

It's nearly eight years, Lyovochka, since you died,
and eight already since I meant to drown myself
in our still pond, the middle one,
where two of your beloved muzhiks drowned—
sister and brother—that long-ago summer. . . .
I feel sometimes that I'm still lying there
beneath the freezing weight of clear water,
staring at a blur of bone-white birch.

Today I visited your grave, no visitor
for once but me, the dark ones and the soldiers
busy preparing for Denikin's troops to come.
The red flag over Yasnaya Polyana
might be white tomorrow—we adapt
past what we think adaptable in us,
survive what seemed beyond survival:
eight years have passed and I am still alive.

But this October I'm like Pushkin's autumn girl—
Today she lives, tomorrow she is gone—
except I haven't her innocence
and hear full well the grave yawning.
I spend most days working for each breath
or dragging this bad leg around the house,
into your study, where I smell you still,
to check your papers for some final fact.

I'd hoped, at least, after the grieving ebbed,
for *silence and slow time,* a quiet stop
between the fallen world and heaven.
But one can't keep life off. You'd weep
to see your ravaged trees, the Red Guards
drilling on the lawn. The house is full
of strangers passing through the halls like ghosts.
How far we were from all that's happening now.

I've made my will, asking forgiveness from,
and forgiving, everyone. Just two nights ago
I gave Tanya the little porcelain cup
that was my mother's final gift to me.
As if I didn't see how futile the gesture,
Sergeenko, the boor, shouts of a new order
in his manic baritone, the morning air so chill
inside the house his words rise up on plumes.

What would he have from us? Sometimes
the Bolsheviks bring flour and good coffee
(one's never quite sure why), and we have weeks
of civility: Weber at night
(that favorite piece of yours) or else the girls
singing. I thought of the old days when you
still had time for tea and *vatrushki—*
small pleasures, necessary pleasures.

But all things sweet went out with your passion
for a program that left no room for life. . . .
Your leaving here was just your way
of wishing yourself dead before you died.
I longed for the pond's cold oblivion,
you for imagination's lone *iszbah*.
It does not exist, my dear husband;
there's no exile from desire's homeland.

A LETTER FROM RYDER

23 April 1898

My Dear Mrs. Warner—

My visit of last week was the occasion
of much pleasure to me: fine company
gathered at table, the chance to see
those ideal girls Rosalie and Frances—
they've grown so fast!—an evening spent
in your kind presence. For all, much thanks.

I am having a common day,
hunger while I paint or rather hunger
instead of painting, but rarely sate myself—
my studio is not, as you've noticed,
a place to savor food, though the smell of linseed
always makes a pear taste better.

Mr. Sherman's paintings in New Bedford
intoxicated more by smell than sight—
the low-tide deliquescence, kelpy, raw,
coming through the open door, mixing
with the pith of turpentine
and glottal oils pressed from tubes.

He'd work his palette like a spinster,
each color separate, preserved and chaste:
mustard yellow, a mercurial red,
pitch-black for his shaky initials,
so carefully placed. I didn't learn from him,
not this precious care at least. . . .

But then you've seen me work, pacing, singing,
covered in pigment, canvas caked with paint,
no order to anything. When Inglis,
dear man, set up that Fifth Ave. studio for me,
I went stale in all its splendor,
used it twice and gave back the key.

From my two windows—I wouldn't trade
for a palace prospect—I watch
with a consumptive stare this brooding sky
(or so I think it broods; perhaps it's only me writ large).
Today no window view, no smell
or measure of singing, gets me anywhere.

I'm working on the Jonah again—
what could I sing?—how many years
have been swallowed up since I began?
You and Olin, God rest his soul, came by,
hellish heat, after your dinner at the Albert.
The Bachelor Boys were kicking around upstairs;

we called them down, talked late, then found
that dank saloon, Fourteenth and Fourth:
some nautical name, of course (I chose it)—
The Belly of the Whale, I'd like to think—
with cheese so sharp it nearly cut your tongue
and amber beer as wry as our late talk.

I was going on about feeling and form,
though I seldom went on at all,
the quiet one of our set, beset
by a too earnest gravity:
"What avails a storm cloud accurate in form
if the storm is not within?"—that sort of thing.

I was keener then on finding words
for my ideas. Then Weir,
a born contrarian and not the soul of temperance,
cut me off and said we had to claim
the Masters' themes, work them through the press
of native genius for the wine to come of age . . .

though he was drinking beer. Then back to me
(I thought he hadn't heard), "Mark your *feeling*
in those forms, dear Albert, then we'll see. . . ."
So each one chose a theme: Olin, Diana,
that fine bronze in which, if I can be so free,
I see a certain grace that is your own.

The man had gifts; how sorely I miss him—
and how much more must you. . . .
I felt again the emptiness last week
without him there, presiding graciously
over a gathering of friends, his loss—
our loss—no matter how we try, inconsolable. . . .

Alden chose the Muse of Music though so rapt
with that girl's face (I never knew her name)
her head sits on one shoulder (or nearly so);
I'd just that day read through Jonah and the whale,
so claimed it for my theme. That night seems long ago,
longer than the ten years' time it's been.

I am patient; art is long. But the muse
won't visit lately and rote alone won't do.
Robert Bruce's spider, on the hundredth cast,
reached the anchoring beam and quickly spun a web,
but I've cast—to mix the metaphor—
on God's waters a thousand times—and nothing.

Yes, yes, my usual anxieties—
"fretting and stewing," as you like to write—
I know the fatality of making
makes the pictures what they are. But how
slow the seasons pass as I watch them pass;
how quickly they pile up in retrospect.

I try to gain perspective—not so easy now
with this hemorrhaging eye—by thinking
all there is to art is *persisting,* waiting
for the paint to fill my canvas.
But even so I find, at times,
my candle's homage to my art snuffed out.

I have spent nights in ecstasies of work—
sleepless, happily so, unable to eat a thing
or take a drop to drink, and if what coaxes
my full brush is passion, it's all
that's passionate to me. *In* me. That's truth.
Without this appetite, I'm left a little dull.

. . . But I'd meant to ask about the girls' perfume.
This new batch seems the best I've conjured up
in years . . . and the studio still smells of it.
De Gay may carp about my using candle grease
to loosen up my paint—he says I'm worst
at caution, when it counts, than any man he's ever seen

(but really I'm too safe—as if a reckless mix
of medium threw caution to the winds!)
yet careful as a chemist when I make
my scents (he says I make no sense).
I use my nose and when it smells so good
I'd eat the air, I call it done.

This letter, too, I'll call done now.
Once more, my thanks for all your kindnesses
and to your girls give my affection.
I hope you'll let me fill a place at dinner
when next you entertain. Until then, I remain,
Yours sincerely,
                    Albert Pinkham Ryder

AN UNCUT SCENE FROM HERR SOMA'S LAST FILM

Take after take, he never gets it right—
different angles, different actors: it doesn't matter.
He cannot recover the image intact
buried deep in the camera's tricky chest.

This stubborn, grainy obsession: Oedipus
fucking his mother on the imperial bed,
the camera locked on his locked jaw, dark hair
sweeping from her turned head. A violent light

strays over the sheets as if it might kindle
the world to ashes. What stays buried keeps
the rest intact, holds off with temperate grace
the desire to tear one's soul out, one's eyes—

how different, his first film, the last sun
trembling in the trees after the children
found their way home: grateful for the image
that appeared, unconceived, appeased, in one take.

Now, half a hundred takes—the fine technology
riots like a heart sick of its single task,
blood catching on the stalled sprockets . . .
as the ill-starred man pushes against her again and again.

HERR SOMA RELATES THE CIRCUMSTANCES OF HIS BREAKDOWN BEFORE MAKING *THE KNIFE IN THE TARN*

The breakdown came months after I should have been out of danger: I had been finished for some time with the most demanding work.

In fact, I had completed by then even the smallest tasks associated with the film—registering the title at the state archives, paying off the bar tab of my notorious cameraman: everything was clear.

I had entered a social season with friends, mostly artists and writers, a few men of business who generously supported the arts, at the spa we came to annually, a visit I always anticipated with great pleasure.

Even the weather that summer was almost uniformly good.

Though I was animated and happy, at times garrulous, for the first weeks, I became soon after nearly aphasic, so at our nightly dinners, even when our number dwindled to six or eight intimates, I would grin vacantly, silent, trying to follow the conversation with a look of engagement.

While it became increasingly impossible for me to speak, I was writing the script that would become my best film.

That was the summer I became an artist—the same summer I went mad: how obvious!

The first physical sign of my collapse was a sore on my tongue.

Though I obsessively worked my tongue against my teeth to determine if the sore showed signs of spreading, it went away readily enough so I presumed it was an anomaly.

When I felt the itch of another coming on, I convinced myself that the condition was the result of a spurious sexual encounter I'd had the week before, the first physical intimacy of any kind in which I'd engaged in over four years.

The young woman was a bohemian—a painter, an actress, "a surrealist," she said—and her advances were not unwelcome although I'm convinced that I would not have pursued her without them.

She was attractive—I'd noticed her several times exiting the women's baths as I entered the men's—but without her obvious, even aggressive, interest my attraction would have been limited to those occasional glimpses at the bathhouse.

I was by then a widower: the source of the anxiety brought on by our sole encounter was not the guilt of personal betrayal but rather a deeper guilt over the idea of intimacy itself.

I had been given for so long to the act of generation only as a maker of films that this more fundamental expression of that impulse filled me with the self-loathing one reserves only for betrayals of the deepest kind.

The idea of sex—the *thought*, not the *act*—was frightful to me.

I fell in love regularly with the stars of my films, young women whom I chose for their look of rural naïveté and robust charm, but loved them only as images: if I had pursued them in a more corporeal way (I never did), it would have ruined what I was working on.

I'd come to need the separation afforded by the camera.

I actually enjoyed being with the young woman at the spa during our brief tryst.

It was only afterwards, but almost immediately afterwards, that I thought back on our lovemaking as a kind of sickness, a sickness that, in turn, sickened me.

Kierkegaard declares in *The Concept of Anxiety* that fear of a disease creates the ideal conditions for it to flourish, a fact that did not alleviate my anxiety over the bodily manifestations of my revulsion.

Even the knowledge of Kierkegaard's idea, like the knowledge of other ideas, did nothing but heighten my self-consciousness, make me irritable, and worsen my condition.

Now, in addition to the physical fear I had already admitted—indeed, given in to in the form of the sores on my tongue—I became incredulous, doubting the mind's ability to do anything but remain locked in this debilitating cycle, abandoning the idea that knowledge could heal, either psychologically or physically, our wounds, though clearly knowledge, or the mind thinking, could create the wounds themselves.

Soon both my elbows, the right more than the left, my left armpit, and the left side of my groin began to itch unbearably, and as I scratched (I couldn't restrain myself, especially at night when I awoke to the burn of the interminable itching) those parts of my body became raw.

At dinner my companions, who had put up with my silences as if they hardly noticed them (in deference to my usual moodiness or out of neglect I cannot say for certain), began to notice me tearing at my elbows under the sleeves of my dinner jacket.

I had been concealing my torment as best I could.

I consulted the spa's doctor, a jovial man with a certain level of intelligence, at the urging of my companions.

I did not tell him that I suspected my condition was brought on by sexual contact; neither did I reveal the condition of my tongue nor the fact that I had lost my appetite.

The doctor had developed a juice fast at the spa, claiming for it, among other benefits, the ability to heal skin irritation: I was to drink prune juice in the morning, apple juice by day, carrot-tomato juice in the evening.

This program, which was to last three days, was to be followed by a forty-eight-hour period during which I could drink only water.

By the final day of the juice fast I was fully delusional, hallucinating, and manic.

The fact that I hadn't eaten anything substantial for days before beginning the fast exacerbated, to a dangerous degree, its effects on the body and, in turn, its effects on the mind.

In my dreams, waking or sleeping—it hardly mattered—I returned again and again to a ruined building.

Only two parallel walls remained.

They were made of brick the color of mercury and formed a long room open above and on either end.

I stood inside the ruin, modern rather than ancient, among broken chandeliers, endless balustrades, and shards of good china with a child who claimed repeatedly that nostalgia could be immediate, an idea he articulated with the animation of someone uttering a thrilling truth.

His claim—what I felt was a banal observation delivered in a ridiculously portentous manner—annoyed me, yet I shook my head in solemn agreement.

Looking up I noticed a woman—the bohemian from the spa—waving to me from a balcony high on the right brick wall.

At first she flirted outrageously, swaying her hips, smiling lasciviously while looking at me over her left shoulder; then suddenly she began to laugh.

The script for the film I had begun before my illness incapacitated me was based on a brief tale collected by a Scandinavian folklorist in the last century.

A young woman, walking to a dance, sees the reflection in a tarn of a man who is away at sea.

The absent sailor's water figure holds out a knife to the woman; she takes it and proceeds to the dance.

Sometime later the sailor returns from his travels and marries the woman.

One day he finds the knife and asks his wife how she came to possess it.

When she relates what transpired on the way to the dance, the man says, "Then it was you who tormented me with your longing that night," and stabs his wife to death.

The story itself is as simple, ostensibly, as it is grim.

It immediately suggested itself to me as a perfect vehicle for the woman from the spa.

After I was well again, or well enough to be released, I found her in a squalid flat on the upper floor of a Kreutzberg building not unlike the ruin in my dream and asked her to play the role of the young wife.

Once in front of my camera—I swear to you!—I felt entirely cured, as if her presence had worked some magic in my malignant blood and brain.

Since making that film, a great success, as you know, I've been healthy as a farm boy.

LEARNING LAS VEGAS

I was sick of it the second day,
calling to hear your voice
on the tape after you'd turned the ringer off.

I'm learning Las Vegas, the boredom
and beatitude of the overbearing;
a Ferris wheel turns slowly

above the Boardwalk, the riders'
clothes sun-stained black and brown,
their bloated hands raised in the gesture

of surrender (the same for fear
as for freedom), fingers sewn tight
against a desert wind. I learn what's real

slowly here, under a sun that cuts
the corners of my eyes, that turns
the mannequins who ride the jerking carts

into real men and wives and kids
no different from the shirt-and-shorts conventioneers,
the millions from the Midwest on pilgrimage:

O Egypt, your blue Nile, they call; O Paris,
your mansard roofs and skeleton of steel;
O Venice, your clean canals and stripe-shirt gondoliers.

The world and time collapse, the miles and hours
all meaningless in what we've scavenged from millennia—
a sleek black pyramid with its single beam of light,

Caesar's permafrost slaves wrapped
in terrible tunics trimmed in gold, cowgirls
in buckskin boots on the move along a new frontier.

The world is here, dead one, a dead world
that you could reign o'er in some air-locked
box of clear plastic, platinum, and rhinestone,

staring out with eyes as empty as mine
or hers, or those of the heavy-lidded losers
calling bets that breed dreams in the chilled air.

Arising from the flat sands that stretch away,
beneath a dawn I haven't broached in sleep,
this burnished opulence and obsolescence.

There's a scarcity of notebooks here,
a quantity of women who refuse your eyes,
like the one who leaves a hotel room

at 5:18 A.M., short skirt,
clean tennis shoes, and lacy ankle socks—
and now that you're not there, not anywhere at all,

I open up the one thick book I find,
a thousand yellow pages filled with ads
for strangers who'll carry roses to a room.

ELEGY

I thought it strange
that he should leave a mannequin
propped against the counter, strange
that plastic in

the single light
left on above the half-full sink
should look so *drained*—and then it hit:
No, not plastic

but flesh: *his* legs
inside the torn fishnet stockings;
his head in a black rubbish bag.
The tightened string—

or was it flex?—
made him a kind of effigy,
like when boys burn Guy Fawkes—
that's what struck me;

odd connection—
the bagged head, bowed, anonymous,
seemed less than real, not anyone
I knew. Not him,

the man I served
who always smiled, said "Good day"
at work when he arrived.
I tried to turn away

but I had seen,
in a pan hanging from a peg,
my face pale as his must have been
inside that bag.

THE RETURN

Past cherubim and flaming sword painted on a barn like a
    tobacco ad,
I make the steep approach to Eden.
Trees close on each side of the road in summer's late profu-
    sion, dense and disordered—
a landscape I once would have calmed with a name.
But I have forsworn naming—my first mistake, divinely sanc-
    tioned.

It is not written in the book how I return after millennia
to this place where no one would guess it began.
I follow antediluvian maps honed in my mind to perfect clarity
but do not recognize the pitch and roll of these foothills
as you would not recognize me in leather sandals, khaki shorts,
    a sweat-stained panama.
I remember fondly the biblical excess of nakedness
but am glad to have given it up, if not entirely by choice.
My clothes are comic, but think of the prototype I've been for
    dire things:
misogynist ruling over Eve
(I never wanted to, believe me; you should have seen the shape
    of her hand as we ate the apple, blameless, equally),
a curse on the land
(each late afternoon before we left I would marvel at the late light—
    gold on green, long before it became cliché. Imagine),
father of murder
(the hard consonant of his name, my worst device; I will never
    repeat it).

We have no will.

He knows all and gives us nothing that isn't shaped by His own
   desire.

Hindsight: His impure delight in marching the animals before me

(I felt power in the naming, and it felt pure; He presided over
   me, how could it be other than pure?)

How could I resist all that symmetry and motion?

I come again to this never-guessed-at Eden and still temptation:

encroaching hickory and scrub brush shake their leaves like
   parchment,

veins forking into glyphs I am meant to translate;

the anachronistic Judas trees flower into betrayal, into metaphor
   beyond their actual petals.

I will resist now as I could not then this appetite for Knowledge,

the seductive pitch of Name.

Soon it will be autumn in Eden. Unimaginable.

I move easily here, the trees putting off and the landscape
   reduced to essence,

shapes of clay and umber made plain.

There is not so much to name—the trees do not mark off the
   distance like history, *like* anything.

Here in Eden, Judas trees are redbud,

not metaphoric, not a betrayal;

and in this season I can see past the apple tree's trunk

to a brook moaning only its original chord, unnamed, unnamable.

CHILDREN AND CIGARETTE

Grouped in the dusk at the station, blameless
and undaunted behind the burn of one shared cigarette,
this circle of children, their wronged can of animate garbage,
its wrappers aloft like some clipped language around their
    shaved heads.
The stubble's sharp under their soft palms—they touch it
and touch it, as if they'll become easy with absence.

Beyond where I'm walking in the dry autumn street,
I watch their close shuffling, immaculate and strict,
how they linger in the seamy waste of light
near a relic locomotive sunk in the parking lot's tar,
close to the tracks and the quaint station
where passengers cross the vanishing point of the past.

These novices don't eye anyone from their collapsed hoods,
through semaphores of kohl painted around their eyes;
nothing from these wind-thin, these vicious beauties,
their fresh dialect of self-regard and abnegation—
whorls of ink, the speared tongue, ring in the hole
of the belly—distant from me, how I'm rooted
in the sobriety of a name, a face, a set of ruling years.

THE TELESCOPE ROOM

What we know of the dark world—the kiss,
the corpse, the fuck, the dream, the fever—
does not refract through the doubled mirror
sleeping in the sealed tube of the brutish

telescope. It is aimed at remote sky,
tilting at the absolute, sighted like a rifle.
Outside, the students riot in the old quadrangle,
smashing their microscopes, demanding the lie

be undone, an account of the new equations
that replace the vivid X's and pretty O's
with the formula for unredeemable zero:
the final proof of their disenchantments.

In the telescope room, its informal
clutter containing his unruly theory,
the calm Professor of Astronomy
cannot hear the young men beyond these walls,

his back to the globe of the old order
stalled on its Empire tripod,
his open books as little help as the lost gods
of redaction who escaped the future's

fate. He keeps company through the night
with an unimaginable chaos
hunched over a sharp German compass,
drawing new circles to appease his sight,

plotting a new quadrant of stars,
its revelation a negativity, an absence,
a small and implacably dense
emptiness pulling the universe to its maw.

PEDAGOGY

You have forced on them the necessity of surprise,
an aesthetic of abandon, the crossed wire of privilege,
as if you yourself possess them—you and your required trespass,
this lighting of fuses alien to your spruce shirt.
Those young are not your tender for transport, aggravant—
not your ruminants, chewing, chewing, on your sharp field of glass;
not your lovers tasting the salt kiss of shapely persuasions.
You're passing them words divisible from knowledge,
words that will stick in their pretty young throats.

OCKHAM

In the nominalist dawn
Ockham walks the edge of the Thames,
content with the present,
the river's flat inland glissando
whole, separate from the need to move
always to the telestic flash of the ocean.

William, you razored the air
thick with golden eyes
spawning in the darkness
down to something manageable.
Behind the fluted tracery's closework
you hacked out essence,
the basic logic,
then thinned to delirium
in Bavarian winter,
an exile starving for air
as bodies drifted in snow
their dark groins fertile with buboes.

Today your shade moves easily
among the students in Oxford,
the ceremony of your gown dark,
no mysteries in the folds.
More like you, they know
each bird flies only in the service of itself,
each bud yields its scent
no farther than their noses.

It is the same dawn
of your hierophantic youth,
inceptor, when the sky, sooted,
lifts only to the pale color of a known star.

ABANDONED HOUSE

We became strangers when we entered the house together,
our boots over the broken glass of last century's fallen sashes,
our boots over the yielding floorboards and their rat-worked plaster.
We entered each room looking for the usual thrill of trespass
(this husk, too, bore its one pale skull like a single kernel of dry corn),
but instead were frightened by a new emptiness in those rooms,
which rendered our lives vacant amidst the drifting flights of
    snow outside.
We were not transported into a past or the memory of
    another's failure,
but instead stood gaping at the black glass—the few panes that
    remained—
mediating the nothing outside and the nothing in there, the glass
that showed no moon but only the sucked reflections of our
    own faces,
the pale features of interlopers who had just become
the newly nameless inhabitants of this lost place.

FRIEZE

The last days were ceremonious,
chaste with the promise of dissolution.
Smoke from our candles passed into dusk
from the porch where we shared good food
and talked as strangers. I was astonished
by the pale light in your face, the cool rehearsal
of our failures, the way we offered words
to one another in some sweet demotic tongue.
We watched stars fix the East in fine grids,
rested our glasses and knives in silence,
victims no longer to the old hunger.
Your Egyptian wrists stalled at beautiful angles;
my knees clasped granite like the Old King's.
Stylized past corruption in faience and gilt,
we passed into the painted kingdoms, the frieze
holding us in absolute abeyance. Canopic
jars bore our viscera in procession to the Hall of Judgment,
a gauze of incense, the largo of pipes.
I learned too late what I could have held back.
Against the Truth, Anubis weighs my heart
featherlight, then tosses it to the demons.

FOR A STREET SINGER

Unable to sleep without her pure corporal solace,
that warmth beyond reason and love that led me
(so willingly) out of myself each night,

I wandered here for the crowds,
everyone busy with one another
in the square's chill September logic.

Your voice, tired by now, tired like I am tired,
stops me. You could be my soul,
soul-small in cut fatigues, the same bleached shirt.

Past you, in the flower-shop window,
the iris, a blur behind glass,
open inside the dark store.

THE VON TROTTA WOODS

Through birch and pine we walk in silhouette,
identical against a void of snow.
We leave a track in silence we cannot follow back.

Mute language rides the cold in plumes.
Lost in rows of winnowed pines that needle into blue,
we flash dark, then light, all panic, all silent motion.

Trunks split around us. We scream in your voice,
then mine, soundless as dream. If I find you
in this landscape of division where all shapes repeat

I will see a face like my face
through air that brings blood to our cheeks,
the only color in this filmed black and white.

LETTER FROM PARIS

New Hampshire summer—scrub brush, pine—
your vague cottage with its one big room
like my one room (or so I picture it)
seems closer here: the strain of proximity
relaxed, resistance gone. Gone too
an old idea that kept alive the order
of our intimacy—so misplaced now,
so past—refusing with its mouth of glass
the words we spoke together: "give" and "take."
Your voice was full, familiar in my ear,
the night before I left. Even through
a silent year the thrill came back, something
like danger, always security courting
the unsafe: the test results, the faith
that felt always like the end of faith.
Unsettled by that feeling you were there
when it was just the phone, as if a look
aside would show your face next to mine.
You gave me facts, not coldly but so felt
I felt again the loss of your refusal
to defend yourself from feeling. You said:
"our" dog, the paper truck, a quick death. . . .
I read tonight, in this old city new to me,
the "Morte d'Arthur," a student's book
left where I was left to spend the night.
Tennyson in Paris—dumb confluence:
But then lines so maudlin that I laughed
to think they raised anything in me:
And I . . . go forth companionless,
And the days darken round me, and the years,

Among new men, strange faces, other minds.
We reached no such dramatic end—nothing
beyond the stubborn vicissitudes
that moved us in some slippery, causal way
toward disowning one another.
Tomorrow I will go to the Beaubourg,
where the Pompidou devours buildings
of the *ancien régime* and find its skeleton
beautiful through the rosette window
of a church, that accommodated contrast
an emblem of our terminal reverse.

AFTER THE DANCE CONCERT

Converted to your religion of pure movement,
I watched from the Surrey's mock Tudor shadow,
a midsummer sky blinking its first benediction.
A haze of insects took blood and moved on,

like you with your boy's hair and livid ankles,
the body between a mark in dense air
I can't focus for desire's guilty lens.
So self-contained, essentially your own,

you left me feeling like I wasn't there
when we sat silent between sips of wine
and talk of Joan of Arc and Saint Jerome—
your incandescent girl, still flesh but burning

toward myth, mobile and unreal,
in the painting at the Met; my saint
all bookishness and loss, the lineman's legs,
a mason's arm—"how much our bodies weigh on us. . . ."

Past your dancer's discipline
a different discipline—or was it only strength?—
lent a perfect ease to those few nights,
as if we'd loved each other years before

or played out friendship in some adult dream
of children's love. We sprawled like kids
across the rug, loose, contented, but,
when we touched, somehow bodiless.

THAW

You burn the winter refuse
in slanting snow, at ease and alert,
past the nimbus of the barrel's rising heat
that erases a white line of fence behind you.
The plane of your willing cheek
resists December's weather,
all gravity and the diagonals of loss,
as you watch, then feed the fire
another length of ripped pilaster
from autumn's half-done renovation.
A still-warm scrim of fallen cinders
melts snow and thaws a patch of dormant grass
as I am thawed by the sight of you
—black cap, red coat, blue jeans—
beyond this window's grid of lights.

THE RESERVOIR

The smell of the reservoir—
its breeding and corruption:
that too was in our heads.

Our limbs across beds
dense with thyme
and the rough tongues of mint,

their needling scents
against the unmaking odor
of the water downhill.

The two of us in the night garden
above that rift of water
filling the dammed-up valley,

its drowned graves and little churches.
The two of us there; the reservoir below:
what's proximate, what's distant.

I envy us that lost August
of our bodies, pale and given
to the sounds of breathing and skin

that silenced our other natures.
In a tangle of stems,
the season's plait of green,

our forgotten selves,
a moon-white leg and length
of back sunk in the loam,

the memory of our shapes
still in the dirt, in the underground hives
made from thaw and ice.

THE HERON

Unlikely haiku: the heron's courtly pose
described against this cold Maine cove

as if some writing-master's brush
had set him there, his too long legs

the last strokes of a character
that's Japanese to me. Hard to see,

a gray not much more blue than rock,
he's barely moved in half an hour.

He trains his eyes on shadows and wake-traces
in the eel-grass shallows, fishing at dusk.

I loll on the porch, the twilight's chill
no longer autumn's augury

but autumn itself. My papers shift—
and I am nearly past the awe

of audience with this ambassador
from some far kingdom of pure form

who won't reveal his emperor's decree.
He hasn't come for me—but as we share

the stasis of this hour and our habits'
solitude, I recognize how instinct

wed to form and the cold eye's
austerity can claim its charm.

My heron draws his neck into an S,
then breaks the water with his beak;

he's got his fish, this mannerist
who's gleaned the contents of the bay.

FIDDLEHEAD FERNS

They mark the April woods in discrete groups,
each head bowed and fixed on the tall father's fern foot. . . .
But, no, they are not human, these spring grotesques,
their stalks lit to the opacity
of skin, the unfurling pod of the fern head
in its stalled, alien gesture of ascent.
Our naming does no good. As if the form
of what a violinist holds brings some measure
of beauty to this raw growth. The notes—
think of Vivaldi's "Spring"—do not redeem
the first and final world of the wet floor
where these mute, unknowing stalks repel us.

LOVIS CORINTH'S *SAMSON BLINDED*

But Lovis, there you are again!
Even behind the blood-soaked bandage
it's clear those are your eyes—
which gave you so much trouble—

and in the ravaged strongman's hands
you've found an image—paint made flesh—
of your own desperate hands.
Past prime an hour, your Samson's well past myth.

His pain, unlike the pain in your bad prose—
its *Sturm und Drang* negating all you felt—
hits bone.
Your late self-portraits will include a skull

but not your hands, their freedom bound
by Samson's chain to artifice,
as if without that prisoner's restraint
you'd raise them against yourself.

JEROME'S DREAM
(after Bellini)

Blue sky clear as your brow, intent, you read
the one true book spread on a crooked tree,
a man in peace, penitent of the wood.
Is this a life, this quarto, leather-bound
with clasps of gold? Ascetic, are you cold?

The afternoon turns toward the evening star
and offers a pale light, past zenith, hard
to read by—as you sleep, a child's cry
outside the circle of your hermitage
breaks the stasis of the vesper hour.

No diatribe against the lure of sex
can drown the human pitch of this baby:
"It's yours—it's yours," a mother whispers.
Then there's nothing of mother or child,
only a white cat keening in the cypress grove.

You show an open hand as if to say,
Come here to me. The cat paces and moans.
You feel a fear beyond your faith.
Get off your knees and run! Your robe,
a beggar's castaway, burns in your wake.

Your thighs, great ashy trees, drop ash
that burns the bridge, flame spreading
bridge to bough, the kindled trees
king-candles promised in Revelation.
Beyond the voice of Rome, pale saint-to-be,

your calling's soot: incinerate your home. . . .
You shudder, start, and wake in sweat. In ink
you dip the cartilage of the quill to write,
in a neat hand, the record of a dream,
a gloss to fill the margin of your book.

ARCADE

We wander through the half-lit corridor
drawn to this display of inwardness and exposure:
tumors atrophied in clouded alcohol, the venereal display
lining the shelves in the Museum of Anatomy;

the buried and diseased, both lure and fear;
the song of the body in the coves and crenellations
of the obsolete architecture's beautiful excess,
once the pride of our famed capital, now the garish

and ungoverned possession of the arcade's transients.
As boys we bought no souvenirs of our great city,
no postcards or the tin of scaled-down monuments,
no tokens of a place we did not recognize as ours.

We crave transport, still scurrilous our disregard
for destination—the travel posters in the kiosk
show black-hulled ships and trains of seamless steel,
the ports or stations where they're bound pure pretext.

We eye the pipes of amber, glowing in their blue felt cradles,
the badger brushes tipped in silver—a Dada dream of women—
the manicure scissors forged in the shape of an ibis flown
from the flickering images in the opticon's profuse darkness

in which we trained our greedy eyes, hot pfennigs in our hands,
to see the world beneath the waking world, the place
to which we will return, unchanged and remade, through the
        opposite arch,
carved ivy and cartouche, identical to the one we entered.

NOTES

"The City" (p. 1)

The artist Frans Masereel was born in Belgium in 1889. Best known for his "novels in woodcuts" such as *Die Stadt* (1925) and *Landschaften und Stimmungen* (1929), Masereel often took as his subject the cities of Berlin and Paris between the wars. His works were banned by the Nazis and widely distributed in Communist countries, though he was never affiliated with any party and rejected the idea of strictly political art. He died in Avignon in 1972. The poems in this sequence respond to images in *Die Stadt*.

"Lovis Corinth at Walchensee" (p. 25)

Between 1918 and 1925, Lovis Corinth (1858–1925) took the alpine lake of Walchensee as the subject of nearly eighty paintings. Approximately forty miles south of Munich, Walchensee lies on what was known as the Italian Road, the route Goethe took south in 1789 when he stopped to sketch a twelfth-century chapel on the lake's southern shore. Corinth writes of Walchensee as the "lake of suicides" and notes that "down in the valley stands a small locked shed in which the victims of the lake are gathered." *Walchensee with Larch* (1921) shows a tree near the shore that Corinth often painted. Horst Uhr's comprehensive and elegant monograph, *Lovis Corinth* (University of California Press, 1990), provides biographical material that appears in this poem. The painting that is the subject of "Lovis Corinth's *Samson Blinded*" (p. 74) is reproduced in Uhr's study.

"Adrian Leverkühn's Song for the Clearwings" (p. 27)

In Thomas Mann's novel *Doctor Faustus,* the composer Adrian Leverkühn flees a brothel after being approached by a prostitute he calls Esmeralda. This name recalls his boyhood fascination with clearwing butterflies (*hetaera esmeralda*), a favorite subject of his father's discussions on natural science.

Returning to the brothel a year later, Leverkühn learns that Esmeralda has gone to Pressburg: "She whose mark he bore had been hidden in a house there, having had to leave her former place for hospital treatment. The hunted hunter found her out." Despite Esmeralda warning him "against her body," Leverkühn insists "upon possession of this flesh" and contracts syphilis. Mann's narrator, Serenus Zeitblom, the composer's biographer and friend, reveals that many of Leverkühn's compositions contain a "a five- or six-note series" derived from the letters of the name *hetaera esmeralda*. (See Thomas Mann, *Doctor Faustus: The Life of the German Composer as Told by a Friend*, translated by H. T. Lowe-Porter [Alfred A. Knopf, 1948].

"A Letter from Ryder" (p. 33)
The American artist Albert Pinkham Ryder (1847–1917) painted most of his seascapes, mythological scenes, and nature studies in his famously cluttered studio on Fifteenth Street in New York City. He was a friend of sculptor Olin Warner who died as the result of a bicycle accident in 1896. After Warner's death, Ryder maintained a "warm and cordial friendship" with the family and kept up a regular correspondence with Sylvia Martinache Warner, the sculptor's widow. I learned a great deal about Ryder's life and work from William Innes Homer and Lloyd Goodrich's *Albert Pinkham Ryder: Painter of Dreams* (Harry N. Abrams, 1989). This book contains a number of interesting appendices, one of which includes selections from Ryder's correspondence (including letters to Mrs. Warner).

"The Von Trotta Woods" (p. 64)
Margarethe Von Trotta's films include *Sisters, or the Balance of Happiness* (1979), *Marianne and Juliane* (1982), *Sheer Madness* (1984), and *Rosa Luxemburg* (1986).

"Arcade" (p. 76)
This poem is indebted to Siegfried Kracauer's discussion of Berlin's *Lindenpassage* in *The Mass Ornament*, translated and edited by Thomas Y. Levin (Harvard University Press, 1995).